Kathy Schrock's
Every Day of the School Year Series

Teaching Science through Literature

Grades 6–8

Nancy J. Keane
Corinne L. Wait

A Publication of Linworth Learning

Linworth Publishing, Inc.
Worthington, Ohio

Library of Congress Cataloging-in-Publication Data

Keane, Nancy J.
    Teaching science through literature, grades 6-8 / Nancy J. Keane, Corinne Wait.
        p. cm. -- (Kathy Schrock's every day of the school year series)
    Includes index.
    ISBN 1-58683-111-9
    1. Science--Study and teaching (Middle school)--United States. 2. Children's literature
in science education--United States. I. Wait, Corinne, 1945- II. Title. III. Series.

Q197 .K43 2002
507'.1'273--dc21

                                                    2002073414

Published by Linworth Publishing, Inc.
480 East Wilson Bridge Road, Suite L
Worthington, Ohio 43085

1-58683-111-9

5 4 3 2 1

Table of Contents

About the Authors

Nancy J. Keane is a school librarian in Concord, New Hampshire. In addition to her work in the school, Nancy also hosts a radio show on WKXL radio in Concord. Kids Book Beat is a monthly show that features children from the area booktalking about their favorite books. The show is live and very unpredictable! Nancy has also authored a children's fiction book and several books on using booktalks.

Nancy is the author of an award-winning Web site *BOOKTALKS – QUICK AND SIMPLE* http://www.nancykeane.com/booktalks. She has set up a discussion list to bring together people who want to discuss booktalking and share booktalks. booktalkers@yahoogroups.com is an open list that welcomes new members.

Nancy received a BA from the University of Massachusetts, Amherst, an MLS from University of Rhode Island and an MA in Educational Technology from George Washington University. She is an adjunct faculty member at New Hampshire Technical College, Connected University, and teaches workshops for the University of New Hampshire.

Nancy lives in Concord, New Hampshire, with her children, Aureta and Alex. They share their home with their dog and four cats.

Corinne L. Wait is a 7th grade language arts teacher in Concord, New Hampshire. Over the past 30 years, Corinne has taught English in grades 7 through 12 and currently teaches middle school language arts.

A cooperative learning trainer for the Concord School District, she has also taught graduate courses in cooperative learning. She has a BA in English and a MEd in curriculum and instruction, with an emphasis on teaching writing and using higher level thinking strategies. Recently, she has been focusing on studying and incorporating best practices in teaching reading.

An avid cook, Corinne enjoys creating meals for her husband and family, especially two-year-old granddaughter Devan.

Acknowledgements

We wish to thank the people who have helped with this endeavor. First, we would like to thank the authors who created these marvelous stories for us to enjoy. With so many children's books in print, it was quite difficult to limit the entries in this book. Without these extraordinary people, this would have been an arduous task.

We would also like to thank the many librarians who have allowed us to use their collections. The library staff of the Concord, New Hampshire, School District has been very helpful. The staff of the Children's Room at Concord Public Library has also been great.

The many wonderful, dedicated teachers we have had the privilege of knowing also influenced this work tremendously. Their ideas for activities and their willingness to share helped a great deal. Thanks especially to our editor, Kathy Schrock. She has been wonderfully supportive during this process.

George and Fred, thanks for the brain cells.

Most of all, we would like to thank our families. Without their support, this book would never have been completed.

A Word from Kathy Schrock

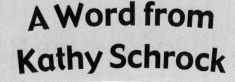

Welcome to the Every Day of the School Year Series. As an educator, library media specialist, and now technology administrator, I know how important it is for the classroom teacher to extend the learning experiences in the classroom. With the current focus on standards-based teaching, learning, and assessment, I felt it was important to supply classroom teachers and library media specialists with activities that directly support the curriculum but at the same time allow for creative teachers to provide supplementary and extension activities for their students.

The activities in this series are varied in scope, but all of them provide practical tips, tricks, ideas, activities, and units. Many of the activities include related print and Internet sites that the classroom teacher can easily collect before engaging in the activity. There are handouts, worksheets, and much more throughout the books.

In my job as technology administrator for a school district, I am often able to plan lessons with teachers and visit classrooms to observe the teaching of the lesson. In addition, as the creator and maintainer, since 1995, of Kathy Schrock's Guide for Educators, http://discoveryschool.com/schrockguide/, a portal of categorized Web sites for teachers, I often receive e-mail from teachers who are searching for practical, creative, and easy-to-implement activities for the classroom. I hope this series and these activities provide just the impetus for you to stretch and enhance your textbook, lesson, and standards-based unit.

If you have any titles you would like to see added to the series, or would like to author yourself, drop me a note at *kathy@kathyschrock.net*.

How to Use this Book

Another school year begins—another stretch of days to work with children. There is something very special about the beginning of the school year. We always look forward to a new year, but also know we need to put together another year of lessons with the students. Using children's literature in the classroom to introduce or extend the classroom lesson is a proven way to get students involved. Using children's literature in the classroom is becoming more and more common. Students often see fiction as more approachable and inviting than nonfiction. One way to excite children about reading is to use booktalks, short book promotions that tease them into wanting to know more. Books that are not promoted often stay on the shelves to collect dust. When children hear about books, either through friends or through booktalks, they are more apt to take them down and read them.

Educators have long known the importance of reading. In 1997, *President Clinton's Call to Action for American Education in the 21st Century* emphasized the importance of reading in the developmental process of children. The document stressed the need for all fourth grade children to be able to read independently. Every state's educational standards also include an emphasis on independent reading as a standard to be addressed. The American Association of School Librarians, a division of the American Library Association, adopted their national standards, *The Information Power Standards*, in 1998. It is clear that the criteria for being an information-literate person involve reading independently and understanding what is read. Students are often drawn towards fiction for their reading choices. If we use fiction as a springboard for learning, they will be able to connect reading for pleasure with reading for information.

This book contains lesson ideas that center on language arts topics. These are all based on children's literature chosen to support a theme. The literature may be a well-known classic or a newly published piece. Children's literature has long been a vital part of every child's life. The stories often reflect society and help the child learn about his or her world. Children's literature exposes students to differing perspectives from which they may experience events in a nonthreatening way. Historical fiction introduces them to what life was like long ago. This helps make history more accessible because it is told in a way understandable to young children. By introducing students to different concepts via fiction, we open the door to exploring topics in greater depth.

The purpose of this book is to promote fiction reading and to encourage the discussion to go further into real-life activities. The chapters are divided into topic areas. Each chapter includes a sample booktalk for that subject. A suggested book list is included and classroom activities follow.

The booktalks are in the form of short teasers to get the students interested in the books. They can be modified to reflect the needs of the population of children and the style of the booktalker. Information included about the book includes the author, title, publisher, date of publication, interest level (IL – given as grade level) and reading level (RL – given as grade level). The booktalk immediately follows this bibliographic information.

The suggested book lists include books that reflect the theme of the chapter. The information given for each book includes author, title, publisher, date of publication, interest level (IL – given as grade level) and reading level (RL – given as grade level). Also included is a short annotation based on the Library of Congress summary statement.

Activities are tied in with each theme. These activities are samples and ideas of the type of things you may want to do with your students in order to follow up and expand upon the theme. They are just starter activities and leave plenty of room for you to personalize the activity for your students. To help with some activities, handouts are included. Some handouts can be copied and passed out to students, while others are grading rubrics for use by the student and teacher.

Most states have adopted educational standards to ensure all students are taught a common curriculum. Standards-based curriculum holds a great potential for student achievement. There are a variety of standards available from national standards to state standards to local standards. For over a decade, the Mid-continent Research for Education and Learning group (McREL) has been a recognized leader in developing K-12 standards for student achievement. Among their contributions to the education field is their compendium of K-12 standards. These standards can be accessed at http://www.mcrel.org. National standards have also been developed by educational organizations. The National Council of Teachers of English has developed standards for England Language Arts. Their website can be accessed at http://www.ncte.org. The National Science Teachers Association has developed national standards for science education. Their website is http://www.nsta.org. And, The National Council for Social Studies has developed standards for Social Studies and can be found on the web at http://www.ncss.org. The International Society of Technology Education has developed The National Educational Technology Standards (NETS) that can be found at http://www.iste.org.

It is hoped classroom teachers, school librarians and media specialists, and public librarians will find inspiration in this book to use booktalking as a starting point for the discussion of themes. When children begin a lesson with enthusiasm, it's sure to be a hit!

To find out more about booktalking and to access a database of ready-to-use booktalks, visit the web page *Booktalks – Quick and Simple* at http://www.nancykeane.com. There is also an electronic discussion list to share and discuss booktalks. To join, simply visit *Booktalks – Quick and Simple* and click on "Join Booktalkers Group" or go to http://groups.yahoo.com/group/booktalkers/

Chapter One

Natural Disasters

Introduction

Middle school students often study weather and the environment as part of the curriculum. The study of natural disasters helps students gain an understanding of the ways in which the natural sources of energy, such as tectonic plate movement and weather systems, affect humans. In response to these forces, humans construct shelters, homes, and buildings to withstand or protect against the forces of nature over which they have little control. In this chapter, we will look at books dealing with natural disasters such as earthquakes, floods, and storms, and discover how the characters from the books survive and cope with their circumstances.

Standards Addressed

Students will be able to explain weather-related phenomena such as thunderstorms, tornados, hurricanes, drought, or acid precipitation. They will demonstrate how living things alter the Earth's atmosphere, lithosphere, and hydrosphere. They will explain how natural hazards and disasters affect the way people live and discuss what types of natural disasters may occur in their community, region, state, nation, and the world. They will be aware of the steps necessary to prepare for a natural disaster.

Sample Booktalk

Cottonwood, Joe. *Quake! A Novel.* New York: Scholastic, 1995. IL 5-8, RL 6.4

I have really been looking forward to Jennie's visit. We were best friends when we were little. She moved away a few years ago but I know we'll just pick up where we left off. After all, we were so incredibly close back then. It really comes as a surprise to me when she arrives. She's just so different from what I remember. And she acts as if she really doesn't want to be here. The only reason she came is that my parents have tickets for the World Series game. Jennie's Mom and my parents are going to the game while Jennie and I babysit for my little brother. Jennie just seems so distant. Even my dog doesn't remember her. When the dog runs out of the house acting as if she was hurt, my brother and I follow. What could be wrong with the dog? When we get outside, it starts. I heard it before I felt it. I felt it before I saw it. It was like a freight train going by right next to me. Only there were no trains around our house. Could this be what I think it is? Yes–it's an earthquake! It's the biggest one I've ever felt. And it's happening when my parents are not home! Travel with Jennie, my brother and me while we find out how life changes when the earth moves.

Book List

Anderson, Laurie Halse. *Storm Rescue.* Middleton, WI: Pleasant, 2001, IL 5-8, RL 5.7
  When a hurricane hits her town, Suniata must face her fears in order to help a stranded cat.

Bodett, Tom. *Williwaw!* New York: Knopf, 1999, IL 5-8, RL 5.9
  In their father's absence, 13-year-old September and her younger brother Ivan disobey his orders by taking the boat out on their Alaska bay, where they are caught in a terrifying storm called a williwaw.

Clark, Billy C. *Riverboy*. Ashland, KY: Jesse Stuart Foundation, 1997, IL 5-8, RL 2.8

Brad finds his loyalties divided when his mother leads the campaign to build a flood wall along the banks of the Big Sandy River—a project his friend, Dan Tackett, an old man who lives in a cabin on the river, calls "pure foolishness."

Garland, Sherry. *The Silent Storm*. San Diego: Harcourt Brace, 1995, IL 5-8, RL 5.5

Thirteen-year-old Alyssa has not spoken since seeing her parents die in a hurricane, and now, three years later, another storm threatens the home she shares with her grandfather on Galveston Island.

Gregory, Kristiana. *Earthquake at Dawn*. San Diego: Harcourt Brace, 1992, IL 5-8, RL 6.3

A fictional account of 22-year-old photographer Edith Irvine's experiences in the aftermath of the 1906 San Francisco Earthquake, as seen through the eyes of 15-year-old Daisy, a fictitious traveling companion.

Hamilton, Virginia. *Drylongso*. San Diego: Harcourt Brace, 1997, 1992, IL 5-8, RL 4.6

As a great wall of dust moves across their drought-stricken farm, a family's distress is relieved by a young man called Drylongso, who literally blows into their lives with the storm.

Higman, Anita. *Texas Twisters*. Austin, TX: Eakin, 1999, IL 5-8, RL 7.0

Two students become friends after doing a research project on tornadoes in their state of Texas.

Jones, Martha Tannery. *Terror from the Gulf: A Hurricane in Galveston*. Dallas, TX: Hendrick-Long, 1999, IL 5-8, RL 7.0

In 1900 in Galveston, Texas, 12-year-old Charlie, who fears the sea because of a boating accident that killed his father, overcomes his personal demons to survive a terrible hurricane.

Kehret, Peg. *Earthquake Terror*. New York: Cobblehill, 1996, IL 5-8, RL 4.2

When an earthquake hits the isolated island in northern California where his family had been camping, 12-year-old Jonathan Palmer must find a way to keep himself, his partially paralyzed younger sister, and their dog alive until help arrives.

Reiss, Kathryn. *Paperquake: A Puzzle*. San Diego: Harcourt Brace, 1998, IL YA

Certain that she is being drawn by more than coincidences into the lives of people living nearly 100 years ago, Violet, who feels like the odd sister in a set of triplets, searches for clues to help her avert an imminent tragedy.

Smith, Roland. *Sasquatch*. New York: Hyperion Paperbacks for Children, 1999, 1998, IL 5-8, RL 5.2

Thirteen-year-old Dylan follows his father into the woods on the slopes of Mount St. Helen, which is on the brink of another eruption, in an attempt to protect the resident Sasquatch from ruthless hunters.

Woodson, Frank. *Mean Waters*. Buena Park, CA: Artesian, 2000, IL 5-8, RL 3.5

Best friends Tom and Billy love to go swimming and canoeing, but Tom loses his nerve after saving a grownup from drowning. During a terrible storm, Tom must overcome his new fear of water in order to save Billy from a flood.

Suggested Activities

Activity #1.1: Weather Trackers

Have students track the weather in a local newspaper or on the National Weather Service's Web site for 14 days. Have them cut out the weather section, including maps and forecasts. Then, have students create a weather journal of actual temperature, barometric pressure, rainfall, and other weather data for each day. Finally, ask students to write a paragraph assessing the accuracy of the forecasts (see Activity #1.1 Handout, page 4).

Activity #1.2: Storm Chasers

Have students draw a series of posters of the United States with typical weather patterns in place. Students could track a storm from the Pacific to the Atlantic Ocean. Be sure students understand why weather moves from west to east.

Activity #1.3: And Now, the Weather

Have students write and perform the script of a local weather report. They could use the personality of a local weather forecaster or create their own. For fun, they could create a commercial for sunscreen, umbrellas, or other weather-related products.

Activity #1.4: Hurricanes vs. Tornadoes

Have students debate the topic "Hurricanes are worse than tornadoes." Assign half the group to research and argue the affirmative and half the negative. Award points for the most fact-based arguments.

Activity #1.5: Fault Lines

Have students create a topographical map of the United States showing fault lines. Students could include major cities, cities, interstate highways, and famous landmarks.

Activity #1.6: CitiDome, Inc.

Have students develop an advertising campaign for a company that builds domes for large cities (see Activity #1.6 Handout, page 5).

Activity #1.1 Handout: Weather Trackers

Name _____ Date_____

Weather Journal Keeper

| **Date:** | **Humidity:** |
| | Source: |

Temperature

High: ____ Low: ____

Other: _____ at time _____.

Comments:

Pressure

_____ Inches Hg at time _____.

__ Rising; __ Falling

Comments:

Precipitation

Rain (R), Snow (S), Sleet (E), Hail (A),
Thunderstorm (T), Freezing Rain (Z),
Drizzle (L), Fog (F)

Precipitation amount: _____

Comments:

Astronomical

Sunrise today: _____

Sunset today: _____

Hours of sunlight: _____

Comments:

Cloud Cover

Clear, Scattered, Broken, Overcast

Remarks, interpretations, predictions, significance:

Name _____ Date_____

CitiDome, Inc.

You are the sales and engineering team from CitiDome, Inc. Your company designs and constructs domes that cover entire cities and protect them from atmospheric disturbances caused by pollution. Your domes keep cities from the effects of ozone depletion and manmade pollutants. Your CEO has just handed you the Gotham City account. You must persuade the city council your company can make Gotham City into a safe, comfortable, productive community.

State at least five **problems** that could be corrected by a CitiDome.

1. _____

2. _____

3. _____

4. _____

5. _____

Below state five reasonable **solutions** addressed by the product.

1. _____

2. _____

3. _____

4. _____

5. _____

Below write a slogan to use on billboards and in radio and TV commercials.

Chapter Two

Science Fiction

Introduction

Science fiction is science future. Today's science fiction is tomorrow's reality. Some of the things science fiction writers of the past wrote about are now fact. Writers such as Jules Verne had an uncanny ability to "see" into the future with amazing accuracy. Students need to be aware of the difference between science fiction and fantasy. In science fiction, the stories have a basis in scientific fact. In this chapter, we will see how the characters come to understand the relationships among society, technology and the individual.

Standards Addressed

Students will demonstrate an increasing understanding of how the scientific enterprise operates. They will formulate questions and use appropriate concepts to guide scientific investigations and to solve real world problems. They will demonstrate an understanding that science knowledge has, over time, accumulated most rapidly after acceptance of major new theories.

Sample Booktalk

Sleator, William. *The Boxes*. New York: Dutton Children's Books, 1998, IL YA

Annie Levi has lived with her aunt for a very long time. Aunt Ruth made it clear she didn't have much use for Annie. The only person in her life who loved Annie was her Uncle Marco. He didn't come to visit very often or stay very long. Aunt Ruth didn't like having him around much. On this visit, Uncle Marco left something in Annie's care. There are two strange boxes hidden in the house now. Uncle Marco made Annie promise never to open the boxes and never to let the two boxes be in the same room. At first Annie did exactly what she was told. But as the days went by, her curiosity got the better of her. It wouldn't hurt just to look at them, would it? The box in the basement looked easier to open. With just a few strokes of a hammer, the box opened. Out popped a strange creature. It looked like a mechanical crab. It scurried into a corner and Annie was too scared to look for it. She quickly left the basement and ran upstairs. What had she done? Why didn't she listen to Uncle Marco? What will happen now? Had she really opened Pandora's box?

Book List

Asimov, Janet. *Norby and The Terrified Taxi*. New York: Walker, 1997, IL 5-8, RL 5.2
  Jeff and Norby travel to Earth where a Manhattan taxi with a robot brain helps them investigate Garc the Great's connection with Computer Prime.

Bawden, Nina. *Off the Road*. New York: Puffin, 2001, 1998, IL 5-8, RL 7.6
  In 2035, eleven-year-old Tom follows his grandfather through the Wall and into the forbidden Wild, where they seek to find his grandfather's boyhood home.

Butts, Nancy. *The Door in The Lake*. Ashville, NC: Front Street, 1998, IL 5-8, RL 4.2
After vanishing without a trace one night during a camping trip, 12-year-old Joey reappears two years later, showing no signs of having aged and carrying memories of a strange light in the sky.

Lasky, Kathryn. *Star Split*. New York: Hyperion Paperbacks for Children, 2001, 1999, IL 5-8, RL 6.0
In 3038, thirteen-year-old Darci uncovers an underground movement to save the human race from genetic enhancement technology.

Lowry, Lois. *Gathering Blue*. Boston: Houghton Mifflin, 2000, IL 5-8, RL 6.3
Lame and suddenly orphaned, Kira is mysteriously removed from her squalid village to live in the palatial Council Edifice. Here she expects to use her gifts as a weaver to do the bidding of the all-powerful Guardians.

Paulsen, Gary. *Escape ; Return ; Breakout*. New York: Delacorte, 2000, IL 5-8, RL 6.0
Having been imprisoned when the Confederation of Consolidated Republics, a foreign power, conquered Los Angeles in 2056, fourteen-year-old Cody escapes and endures hardship to become the underground hero named the White Fox.

Philbrick, W. R. *The Last Book in the Universe*. New York: Blue Sky Press, 2000, IL 5-8, RL 6.0
After an earthquake has destroyed much of the planet, an epileptic teenager nicknamed Spaz begins the heroic fight to bring human intelligence back to the Earth of a distant future.

Pinkwater, Daniel Manus. *Lizard Music*. New York: Bantam Doubleday Dell Books for Young Readers, 1996, 1976, IL 5-8, RL 6.9
When left to take care of himself, a young boy becomes involved with a community of intelligent lizards who tell him of a little-known invasion from outer space.

Skurzynski, Gloria. *The Virtual War*. New York: Simon & Schuster Books for Young Readers, 1997, IL 5-8, RL 6.5
In a future world where global contamination has necessitated limited human contact, three young people with unique genetically engineered abilities are teamed up to wage a war in virtual reality.

Sleator, William. *The Duplicate*. New York: Puffin, 1999, 1988, IL 5-8, RL 6.5
Sixteen-year-old David, finding a strange machine that creates replicas of living organisms, duplicates himself and suffers the horrible consequences when the duplicate turns against him.

Waugh, Sylvia. *Space Race*. New York: Delacorte, 2000, IL 5-8, RL 5.7
When he learns he and his father must soon leave Earth, 11-year-old Thomas Derwent is upset. However, a terrible accident separates the two of them and makes Thomas's situation much worse.

Suggested Activities

Activity #2.1: Recycled Robots

Have students create "robots" out of things that can easily be found around the home, such as towel rolls, buttons, and the like. They should include information about the purpose and abilities of each robot.

Activity #2.2: Zero Gravity Sports

Have students rewrite the rules of a favorite ball game so it can be played in zero gravity. How would they account for the ball hovering in the air? What about players leaping effortlessly around the field? What restrictions would be placed on the players?

Activity #2.3: Life in the Future

Have students create a map of what their town will look like in the year 3000. Which landmarks will change, which will disappear, and which will remain the same? What new features will there be? Will bridges be replaced and will roads be changed? What will happen to the parks, shopping areas, schools? What will be the mode of transportation? Have students use details to support why they believe these changes will take place.

Activity #2.4: Earth of the Future

Have students write a scene for their own science fiction movie about a future on earth after a devastating nuclear war. Is there a stable government? Who will run it? Is it a democracy? What kinds of work do people do? What do families, schools, and recreation look like? Will there be a shift in the location of the population? Will there be places where no one can live?

Activity #2.5: Science Fiction or Reality?

Students love to make connections to their lives, to books they have read, and to movies they have seen. Have students create a two-column notebook. On the left ask them to record several quotes from the book that remind them of something else. One quote should relate to their personal lives, one to another book or story, one to a film, and another to a current event. On the right, ask students to write a paragraph explaining each connection (see Activity #2.5 Handout, page 10).

Activity #2.6: To Clone or Not to Clone (Rubric)

Have students write an opinion piece about cloning. Should animals be cloned? What about stem cell research? To what extent should science continue with these issues? What if cures for diseases could be developed? (see Activity #2.6 Handout, page 11).

Name _____ Date _____

That Reminds Me

Quote From Book	Explain Connection

Activity #2.6 Handout: To Clone or Not to Clone (Rubric)

Name _____ Date _____

To Clone or Not to Clone

CATEGORY	4	3	2	1
Main Idea	There is one clear, well-focused main idea.	Main idea is somewhat clear.	The main idea is unclear.	There is more than one broad idea.
Topic Support	High quality relevant details go beyond the obvious or predictable.	Supporting details and information are relevant, but not all ideas are supported.	Supporting details and information are relevant, but many ideas are unsupported.	Supporting details are missing or not related to the topic.
Introduction	The introduction is contains a catchy lead, states the main topic, and previews the paper's structure.	The introduction states the main topic and previews paper's structure, but is uninteresting.	The introduction states the main topic, but does not preview paper's structure and is uninteresting.	There is no clear introduction of the main topic or preview of the paper's structure.
Logical Order	Interesting details are placed in a logical, order.	Details are placed in a logical order, but are uninteresting.	Some details are not in a logical or expected order.	Many details are illogically organized.
Transitions	A variety of thoughtful transitions are used to clearly show connections between ideas.	Transitions clearly show connections, but are not varied.	Some transitions are clear, but others make fuzzy connections.	There are few, unclear, or no transitions between ideas.
Conclusion	The conclusion is strong and clearly paraphrases the theme.	The conclusion is recognizable.	The conclusion is unclear.	There is no clear conclusion.
Sentence Structure	All sentences are varied and well constructed.	Most sentences are well-constructed, but not varied.	Some sentences are well-constructed, but not varied.	Sentences lack structure and appear incomplete or rambling.
Argument	The writer successfully uses several reasons/appeals to engage the reader.	The writer uses several reasons/ appeals to try to engage the reader.	The writer attempts, unsuccessfully, to engage the reader.	The writer makes little attempt to engage the reader.
Grammar, Spelling, Punctuation & Capitalization	Grammar, spelling, capitalization, and punctuation contain no errors.	Grammar, spelling, capitalization, and punctuation contain 1-2 errors.	Grammar, spelling, capitalization, and punctuation contain 3-4 errors.	Grammar, spelling, capitalization, and punctuation contain many errors.

Chapter Three

Survival

Introduction

How do people survive? How do they live in a harsh environment? The study of survival helps students understand how the human body reacts to difficult conditions and how one must draw on one's inner strength to prevail. We can never know just when we may find ourselves in a position that requires us to perform above and beyond the ordinary. In this chapter, we meet several people who are faced with situations that require them to dig deeply and find their true character.

Standards Addressed

Students will describe/identify major organ systems of the human body, state their major functions, and describe some of their interactions, e.g. the heart and lungs working together in respiration. They will explain how the human body remains healthy and fights-off disease, i.e. the immune system, the influence of diet, food and exercise, the influence of microorganisms (bacteria, viruses, protista). They will be able to describe the steps necessary to survive in the wilderness and other inhospitable environments.

Sample Booktalk

Myers, Edward. *Climb or Die*. New York: Hyperion, 1996, IL 5-8, RL 5.5

The trip starts out like many others before it. Danielle and her brother Jake squabble in the back seat while Dad and Mom talk in the front seat. It is October, and they are heading up to their cabin in the Rockies. The two kids are happy with the move to Colorado. It is certainly different from their old home in New Jersey. The snow beginning to fall makes it hard to see. Dad guesses it is just a sudden squall so he continues to drive. When they see other cars pulling off the road, Mom suggests they do the same. But Dad is determined. He will get them through to the cabin. He knows a shortcut. He'll get off the highway and take an old mining road that will get them there faster. The snow is coming down so hard they can barely see out the front window. Suddenly, there is a jolt and the family is thrown around the car. It takes a few minutes to understand what has happened. The car has gone off the road and struck a tree. Dad and Mom are hurt. The kids are shaken up but fine. After spending the night in the car, they come to realize it will be up to Danielle and Jake to go for help. They think they are about 20 miles from the highway. How can they possibly walk that far in foot-deep snow? Or will Jake come up with a better idea? Jake has always been good at improvising and finding solutions to impossible problems. Will he be able to do it this time? Find out why they must *Climb or Die*.

Book List

Farmer, Nancy. *A Girl Named Disaster*. New York: Orchard Books, 1996, IL 5-8, RL 5.9
  While journeying to Zimbabwe, 11-year-old Nhamo struggles to escape drowning and starvation and, in doing so, comes close to the luminous world of the African spirits.

Hobbs, Will. *Far North*. New York: Morrow Junior Books, 1996, IL 5-8, RL 6.8
After the destruction of their float plane, 16-year-old Gabe and his Dene friend, Raymond, struggle to survive a winter in the wilderness of the Northwest Territories of Canada.

Lawrence, Iain. *The Wreckers*. New York: Delacorte, 1998, IL 5-8, RL 4.2
Shipwrecked after a vicious storm, 14-year-old John Spencer attempts to save his father and himself while also dealing with an evil secret about the Cornish coastal town where they are stranded.

London, Jack. *The Call of the Wild*. New York: Tor, 1990, IL 5-8, RL 6.0
Jack London's classic tale tracing Buck's entry into the wild and survival among the wolves.

Napoli, Donna Jo. *Stones in Water*. New York: Dutton Children's Books, 1997, IL 5-8, RL 6.5
After being taken by German soldiers from a local movie theater along with other Italian boys including his Jewish friend, Roberto is forced to work in Germany. He escapes into the Ukrainian winter before desperately trying to make his way back home to Venice.

O'Dell, Scott. *Island of the Blue Dolphins*. Boston: Houghton Mifflin, 1990, IL 5-8, RL 5.5
Left alone on a beautiful but isolated island off the coast of California, a young Indian girl spends 18 years not only merely surviving through her enormous courage and self-reliance, but also finding a measure of happiness in her solitary life.

Paulsen, Gary. *Hatchet*. New York: Atheneum Books for Young Readers, 1987, IL 5-8, RL 6.3
After a plane crash, 13-year-old Brian spends 54 days in the wilderness, learning to survive with only the aid of a hatchet given him by his mother. He also learns how to survive his parents' divorce.

Smith, Roland. *Thunder Cave*. New York: Hyperion Paperbacks for Children, 1997, IL 5-8, RL 5.2
Determined, after his mother's accidental death, to foil his stepfather's plans for his future, 14-year-old Jacob travels alone to Africa in search of his father, a biologist studying elephants in a remote area of Kenya.

Speare, Elizabeth George. *The Sign of the Beaver*. Boston: Houghton Mifflin, 1983, IL 5-8, RL 5.7
Left alone to guard the family's wilderness home in 18th century Maine, a boy is hard-pressed to survive until local Indians teach him their skills.

Taylor, Theodore. *Timothy of the Cay*. San Diego: Harcourt Brace, San Diego: 1993, IL 5-8, RL 6.1
Having survived being blinded and shipwrecked on a tiny Caribbean island with the old black man Timothy, 12-year-old white Phillip is rescued and hopes to regain his sight with an operation. Alternate chapters follow the life of Timothy from his days as a young cabin boy.

Vanasse, Deb. *Out of the Wilderness*. New York: Clarion, 1999, IL 5-8, RL 5.2
Josh tries to endure living in the Alaskan wilderness with his father and half-brother Nathan, but Nathan's uncompromising reverence for nature and its wild creatures causes difficulties that reinforce Josh's determination to return to city life.

Suggested Activities

Activity #3.1: Transportation

Have students replicate a method of transportation that would be useful to the character in the book. For example, students could make snowshoes out of string and oak tag or a canoe out of clay.

Activity #3.2: Survival Necessities

Have students create a graphic organizer of things necessary for survival in the family car. Included should be water, ways to keep warm, high-energy foods, and a signaling device (see Activity #3.2 Handout, page 16).

Activity #3.3: Get the Picture (Rubric)

Have students draw a poster of an important setting in the book including all the physical features such as elevation, vegetation, roads or trails, and climate (see Activity #3.3 Handout, page 17).

Activity #3.4: Biome Diorama

Have students research and create a diorama of the biome in the book. Landforms, plants, and animals should be represented as accurately as possible.

Activity #3.5: Ecologist's Notebook

Have students research and make a scientific journal of all the flora and fauna of the biome in the book. Accurate drawings and descriptions, as well as bibliographic citations for the information, should be included.

Activity #3.6: "I AM" Survival Poem

As the main character, students write an "I AM" poem (see Activity #3.6 Handout, page 18).

Activity #3.2 Handout: Survival Necessities

Name _____ Date _____

On The Road

Fill in the things your family might need to keep in your car to survive being stranded on the road.

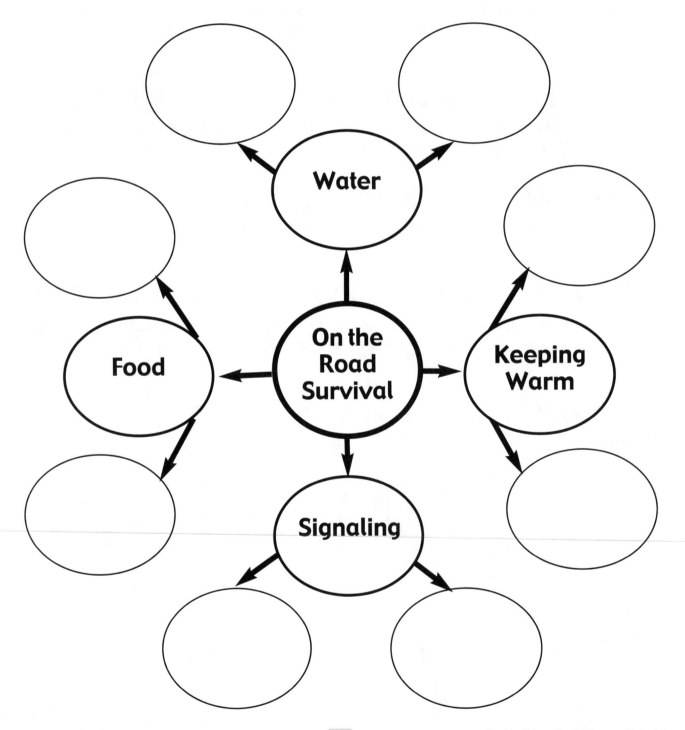

Activity #3.3 Handout: Get the Picture (Rubric)

Name _____ Date _____

Making a Poster Rubric

CATEGORY	4	3	2	1
Graphics — Originality	Several of the graphics used on the poster reflect an exceptional degree of student creativity in their creation or display.	One or two of the graphics used on the poster reflect student creativity in their creation or display.	The graphics are made by the student, but are based on the designs or ideas of others.	No graphics made by the student are included.
Graphics — Relevance	All graphics are related to the topic and make it easier to understand.	Most graphics are related to the topic and most make it easier to understand.	Some graphics relate to the topic.	No graphics relate to the topic.
Required Elements	The poster includes all required elements as well as additional information.	All required elements are included on the poster.	All but one of the required elements are included on the poster.	Several required elements are missing.
Labels	All items of importance on the poster are clearly labeled with labels that can be read from at least 3 feet away.	Almost all items of importance on the poster are clearly labeled with labels that can be read from at least 3 feet away.	Several items of importance on the poster are clearly labeled with labels that can be read from at least 3 feet away.	Labels are too small to view or the important items are not labeled.
Content — Accuracy	At least 8 important benefits are displayed on the poster.	5-6 important benefits are displayed on the poster.	4 important benefits are displayed on the poster.	Less than four important benefits are displayed on the poster.
Attractiveness	The poster is exceptionally attractive in terms of design, layout, and neatness.	The poster is attractive in terms of design, layout, and neatness.	The poster is acceptably attractive though it may be a bit messy.	The poster is distractingly messy or very poorly designed. It is unattractive.

Name _____ Date _____

"I AM" POEM

Pretend you are the main character in your book. You will write a poem to tell the world what you see, hear, think and feel. Use this sheet to draft your ideas. When you have finished, share with a partner, and revise.

I AM

I am a (boy/girl) who must (write the character's goal)

_____

_____

But (write the problem here)

_____

_____

I see

_____

_____

I hear

_____

_____

I feel

_____

_____

I wish

_____

_____

I believe

_____

_____

I know

_____

_____

I am (character's name) _____

Chapter Four

Archaeology

Introduction

Man has always been fascinated with what came before. Where did we come from? How did we get here? In recent history, we have written documents detailing events that shaped our civilization. Before the written word, man preserved knowledge through the oral tradition. We do not have access to many of those old stories, so we must find other ways to discover our distant past. Archaeologists take that task to heart. They use the record found in the rocks to tell the story of early man. By looking at fossils and scattered remnants of times gone by, archaeologists can try to discover things about the lives of those who have gone before.

Standards Addressed

Students will define and describe various physical models and their uses, e.g. cell model, skeleton system. They will recognize that a model is a representation of an object or process and is not identical to the object or process. They will understand how archaeologists search for clues to our past. They will recognize the tools and methods involved in the search.

Sample Booktalk

Jennings, Richard W. *The Great Whale of Kansas.* **Boston: Houghton Mifflin, 2001, IL 3-6, RL 5.8**

For me, there is nothing like digging a hole. I can't tell you why. I just love the feeling of holding a shovel and digging into the earth. There is nothing more worth doing than simply digging a hole. I live in Kansas–Melville, to be precise. If you think of America as a dartboard, Melville would be the bull's eye. We are smack dab in the middle of the country, as far from any ocean as you can get. There isn't much here as far as holes go. There aren't any lakes or rivers around us. So, for my birthday, my parents bought me a pond building kit! I couldn't wait until the weather became nice enough for me to start digging my pond. It came with a video that told all about it and I watched that video every night. I've watched it so many times I have it memorized! When the weather was finally nice enough for me to start building my pond, I spent all my spare time digging. But one day, I hit something hard. It looks like a giant bone. I'd dig some more and gradually the giant creature was exposed. Even though the state museum offers to help dig out the creature, I know it is up to me to carefully uncover what lies in my yard. I've read enough about excavations to believe I can do it. But what will I find? Is it possible I've come upon a whale? In the middle of Kansas? Come along with me and find out.

Book List

Carson, Drew. *Summer Discovery.* Kansas City, MO: Landmark Editions, 1998, IL 3-6, RL 2.8
  While building a fort near their home by the Oregon's Umpqua River, two nine-year-olds make a discovery
  that involves their neighbors in trying to stop a bridge from being built on an important archaeological site.

Conrad, Pam. *My Daniel*. New York: HarperColllins, 1989, IL 5-8, RL 6.1
Ellie and Stevie learn about a family legacy when their grandmother tells them stories of her brother's historical quest for dinosaur bones on their Nebraska farm.

Crichton, Michael. *Jurassic Park: A Novel*. New York: Knopf, Distributed by Random House, 1990, IL YA
An account of the attempt, through a hair-raising 24 hours on a remote jungle island, to avert a global emergency—a crisis triggered by today's rush to commercialize genetic engineering.

Dickinson, Peter. *A Bone from a Dry Sea*. New York: Bantam Doubleday Dell Books for Young Readers, 1992, IL YA
In two parallel stories, an intelligent female member of a prehistoric tribe becomes instrumental in advancing the lot of her people. The daughter of a paleontologist is visiting him on a dig in Africa when important fossil remains are discovered.

Howarth, Lesley. *The Pits*. Cambridge, MA: Candlewick, 1996, IL YA.
After his daughter discovers the Iceman, an eminent archaeologist theorizes about Stone Age culture, greatly irritating someone who was alive in 7650 B.C.

Lasky, Kathryn. *The Bone Wars*. New York: Morrow Junior Books, 1988, IL 5-8
In the mid-1870s, young teenage scout Thad Longsworth, blood brother to the Sioux visionary Black Elk, finds his destiny linked with that of three rival teams of paleontologists searching for dinosaur bones, as the Great Plains Indians prepare to go to war against the white man.

Peters, Elizabeth. *He Shall Thunder in the Sky: An Amelia Peabody Mystery*. New York: William Morrow, 2000, IL YA
Intrepid archaeologist/sleuth Amelia Peabody and her family, back in Egypt in 1914 for another season of archaeological excavation, become caught up in the political turmoil sweeping the country. When an exquisite artifact from a Giza dig is found where it ought not be, Amelia realizes her villainous arch-nemesis, Sethos, is at work.

Stanley, Diane. *A Time Apart*. New York: Morrow Junior Books, 1999, IL 5-8, RL 6.3
While her mother undergoes treatment for cancer, 13-year-old Ginny is sent to live with her father in England, where she becomes part of an archaeological experiment to investigate life during the Iron Age.

Starnes, Gigi. *Grandma's Tales: Storm of Darkness*. Austin, TX: Eakin Press, 1995, IL 3-6, RL 5.5
Jen and her friend Darcey go on an archaeological dig in southern Texas where Jen's grandmother is the head archaeologist.

Yager, Fred. *Rex: A Novel*. Stamford, CT: Hannacroix Creek Books, 2002, IL 5-8, RL 5.9
When he begins to search for his missing paleontologist parents, a young boy finds himself in possession of something long-believed to be extinct.

Suggested Activities

Activity #4.1: Time Line—Planet Earth (Rubric)

Have students create a time line of earth from the Paleozoic era to the present. Students should label the era, period, number of years' duration, and the characteristic life present during each period (see Activity #4.1 Handout, page 22).

Activity #4.2: Geologist

Have students research an important geologist and gather data on his or her education, specialty, and findings. Students will report orally to the class.

Activity #4.3: Archaeologist or Paleontologist?

What is the difference between an archaeologist and a paleontologist? Students research the question and present their findings via a Venn diagram (see Activity #4.3 Handout, page 23).

Activity #4.4: Archaeology and Ethics

What is more important: a culture's beliefs, religion, history, or scientific knowledge? Should archaeologists be allowed to dig up the bones of ancient peoples? What if the results could answer important questions or even find a cure for disease? Students write a thought piece to answer the questions.

Activity #4.5: Archaeology Vocabulary

Have students create a glossary of important terms found in the book. Students should record the word, page on which it was found, the sentence in which it appears, and a dictionary definition (see Activity #4.5 Handout, page 24).

Activity #4.6: Digging Up the Past

Have students take on the role of archaeologists of the future. Have them create a field guide for their team to help them understand artifacts of today (see Activity #4.6 Handout, page 25).

Activity #4.1 Handout: Time Line—Planet Earth (Rubric)

Name _____ Date _____

Time Line—Planet Earth Rubric

CATEGORY	4	3	2	1
Facts	All events are accurately recorded.	Most events are accurately recorded.	Some of the events are accurately recorded.	Events are often inaccurately recorded.
Readability	The time line is pleasing and easy to read.	The time line is somewhat pleasing and easy to read.	The time line is relatively readable.	The time line is difficult to read.
Title	The title is creative and accurate.	The title is accurate.	The time line has a title.	The title is missing or difficult to see.
Dates	Dates are accurate and complete for each event.	Dates are accurate and complete for most events.	Dates are accurate and complete for many events.	Dates are inaccurate or missing for many events.
Spelling and Capitalization	Spelling and capitalization are accurate.	Spelling and capitalization are mostly correct.	Some spelling and capitalization errors are made.	There are many spelling and capitalization errors.

Name _____ Date _____

Archaeologist or Paleontologist?

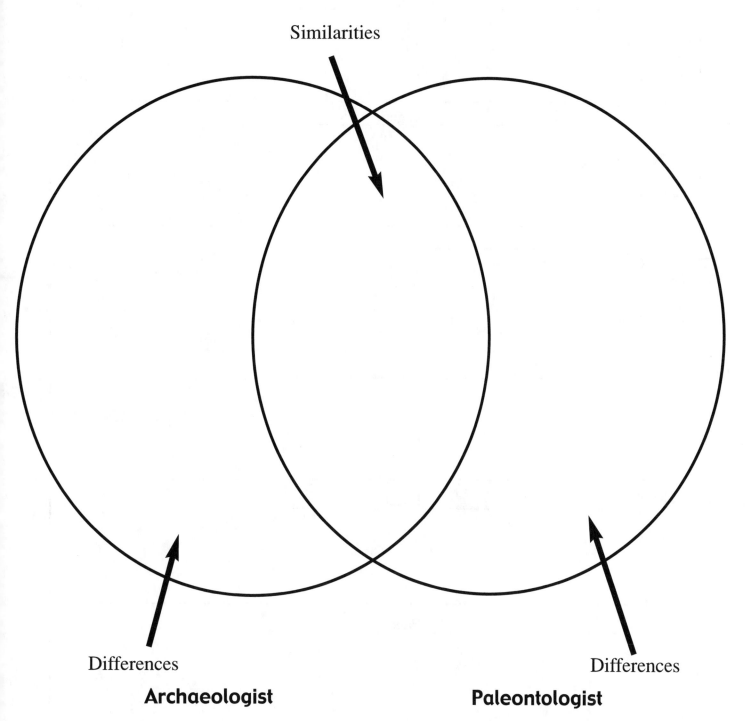

Similarities

Differences

Differences

Archaeologist

Paleontologist

What is the difference between an archaeologist and a paleontologist?

Activity #4.5 Handout: Archaeology Vocabulary

Name _____ Date _____

Archaeology Vocabulary

Word:_____ **Page:**_____

Sentence:

Definition:

Word:_____ **Page:**_____

Sentence:

Definition:

Word:_____ **Page:**_____

Sentence:

Definition:

Word:_____ **Page:**_____

Sentence:

Definition:

Word:_____ **Page:**_____

Sentence:

Definition:

Word:_____ **Page:**_____

Sentence:

Definition:

Name _____ Date _____

Archaeologist's Field Guide

Many years ago, in the twenty-first century, the ancients had strange devices. For instance, a "book" was made of "paper," fibrous material on which words were "printed." This was the quaint device they used for educating the young in large edifices called "schools." Your task is to choose several of these devices and explain their use to people of today's world.

Artifact_____ Purpose _____

_____

Artifact_____ Purpose _____

_____

Artifact_____ Purpose _____

_____

Artifact_____ Purpose _____

_____

Artifact_____ Purpose _____

_____

Artifact_____ Purpose _____

_____

Artifact_____ Purpose _____

_____

Chapter Five

Manmade Disasters

Introduction

Nature is not alone in wreaking havoc on mankind. Humans themselves can cause tremendous damage. Sometimes the danger is known but the risk seems small. Sometimes the danger is entirely unknown with no way to predict disastrous outcomes. The stories in this chapter demonstrate how things people do to make the world a better place may also hurt the environment and threaten life.

Standards Addressed

Students will demonstrate an increasing ability to understand that science and technology can affect individuals, and that individuals in turn can affect science and technology. Students will describe immediate and long-term consequences of various alternative solutions for science and/or technology related issues, e.g. natural catastrophes, interactions of populations, resources and environment, health and disease. Students will determine how technology affects their lives and predict how it might affect their future.

Sample Booktalk

Hesse, Karen. *Phoenix Rising*. New York: H. Holt, 1994, IL 5-8, RL 4.8

The unthinkable has happened. A leak in the nuclear power plant sends radiation throughout New England. People are getting very ill and dying. Nyle and her grandmother stay on their farm in Vermont and do the only thing that they can: hope the wind will continue to blow east and keep them safe. To safeguard themselves, they use protective masks when they tend the sheep. Gran decides to take in two victims of the terrible accident. Nyle does not want to get to know these people because she is afraid they will die soon. What will she learn as she gets to know 15-year-old Ezra? Can she overcome her fear of death and help the victims of the accident?

Book List

Anastasio, Dina. *The Case of the Glacier Park Swallow*. Niwot, CO: Roberts Reinhart, 1994, IL 5-8, RL 5.4
  Finding an injured sparrow with a metal band around one leg is the start to a mystery that takes Juliet Stone from Glacier National Park to Yellowstone, then to Edmonton, Alberta, on the trail of a drug smuggling ring.

Brouwer, Sigmund. *Cobra Threat*. Nashville: Tommy Nelson, 1998, IL 5-8, RL 6.1
  After discovering tainted water in the creek near his grandmother's cabin in the Kentucky hills, senior Roy Linden slowly uncovers a connection between his high school team's new star quarterback, his own football future, and the source of the pollution.

DeFelice, Cynthia C. *Lostman's River*. New York: Avon, 1995, IL 5-8, RL 5.4
  In the early 1900s, thirteen-year-old Tyler encounters vicious hunters whose actions threaten to destroy the Everglades ecosystem and, as a result, joins the battle to protect that fragile environment.

George, Jean Craighead. *Who Really Killed Cock Robin? An Ecological Mystery*. New York: HarperTrophy, 1992, 1991, IL 5-8, RL 6.1
Eighth-grader Tony Isidoro follows a trail of environmental clues in an attempt to determine what ecological imbalances might have caused the death of the town's best-known robin.

Golding, William. *Lord of the Flies: A Novel*. New York: Perigee, 1954, IL YA
Stranded on an island while an atomic war destroys the rest of the world, a group of young boys revert to savagery as they struggle to survive.

Howarth, Lesley. *Weather Eye*. Cambridge, MA: Candlewick, 1997, IL YA
In England in 1999, thirteen-year-old Telly organizes her fellow climate observation club members to calm the planet's turbulent weather.

O'Brien, Robert C. *Z for Zachariah*. New York: Aladdin Paperbacks, 1987, 1974, IL YA, RL 5.6
After living alone for a year, believing herself to be the only survivor of a nuclear holocaust, 16-year-old Ann makes the startling discovery that a scientist named John Loomis has also survived, but this pleasant surprise very quickly turns sinister.

Skurzynski, Gloria. *The Virtual War*. New York: Simon & Schuster Books for Young Readers, 1997, IL 5-8, RL 6.5
In a future world where global contamination has necessitated limited human contact, three young people with unique genetically engineered abilities are teamed up to wage a war in virtual reality.

Taylor, Theodore. *The Bomb*. San Diego: Harcourt Brace, 1995, IL 5-8, RL 6.8
In 1944, when the Americans liberate Bikini Atoll from the Japanese, 14-year-old Sorry Rinamu does not realize that in two years he will lead a desperate effort to save his island home from a much more deadly threat.

Winton, Tim. *Lockie Leonard, Scumbuster*. New York: M.K. McElderry, 1999, IL 5-8, RL 6.7
When Lockie Leonard wipes out on a huge wave, he is thrown into a friendship with the weird but extremely intelligent "Metal Head," Geoff "Egg" Eggleston, who joins Lockie in his crusade to clean up the pollution in his coastal Australian town's harbor.

Suggested Activities

Activity #5.1: Clean Water

Have students research a local body of water that has been cleaned up since the Clean Water Act of 1972. Have students report findings on a before-and-after poster that shows conditions before and after the cleanup (see Activity #5.1 Handout, page 30).

Activity #5.2: TV News

Have students write a script and perform a TV newscast reporting a toxic chemical spill on a major highway during the morning rush hour commute.

Activity #5.3: Nuclear Fission

Have students create a flow chart describing the process of nuclear fission.

Activity #5.4: Non-Polluting Cars

Have students design and draw a non-polluting car. What is the power source that could run the car? What would the car look like? What is it called? Show results by designing a magazine advertisement.

Activity #5.5: Nuclear Clouds

Have students study prevailing winds around the globe and explain graphically how long it would take for a nuclear cloud to travel around the world.

Activity #5.6: Super Kid

Have students create a "super kid" through genetic engineering. The character will need the skills and abilities to survive in a future world (see Activity #5.6 Handout, page 31).

Activity #5.1 Handout: Clean Water

Name _____ Date _____

CATEGORY	4	3	2	1
Before and After Poster				
Graphics—Originality	Several of the graphics used on the poster reflect an exceptional degree of student creativity in their creation or display.	One or two of the graphics used on the poster reflect student creativity in their creation or display.	The graphics are made by the student, but are based on the designs or ideas of others.	No graphics made by the student are included.
Graphics—Relevance	All graphics are related to the topic and make it easier to understand.	Most graphics are related to the topic and most make it easier to understand.	Some graphics relate to the topic.	No graphics relate to the topic.
Required Elements	The poster includes all required elements as well as additional information.	All required elements are included on the poster.	All but one of the required elements are included on the poster.	Several required elements are missing.
Labels	All items of importance on the poster are clearly labeled with labels that can be read from at least 3 feet away.	Almost all items of importance on the poster are clearly labeled with labels that can be read from at least 3 feet away.	Several items of importance on the poster are clearly labeled with labels that can be read from at least 3 feet away.	Labels are too small to view or the important items are not labeled.
Content—Accuracy	At least 8 important benefits are displayed on the poster.	5-6 important benefits are displayed on the poster.	4 important benefits are displayed on the poster.	Less than four important benefits are displayed on the poster.
Attractiveness	The poster is exceptionally attractive in terms of design, layout, and neatness.	The poster is attractive in terms of design, layout, and neatness.	The poster is acceptably attractive though it may be a bit messy.	The poster is distractingly messy or very poorly designed. It is unattractive.

Name _____ Date _____

Super Kid

Reason needed

Reason needed

Reason needed

Reason needed

Reason needed

One of
his or her
characteristics

Super Kid

One of
his or her
characteristics

Reason needed

Reason needed

One of his or her
characteristics

Reason needed

Reason needed

Reason needed

Chapter Six

Ecology

Introduction

The study of ecology in the middle grades emphasizes the relationship between man and the environment. Students study endangered species and learn about ways to protect them. The students also learn the importance of ecological diversity. When business interests and environmental interests clash, students must be able to look at both sides of the issue and be able to weigh the consequences in order to make intelligent, informed decisions. In this chapter, we look at novels dealing with environmental topics.

Standards Addressed

Students will demonstrate an increasing ability to understand how environmental factors affect all living systems (i.e. individuals, community, biome, the biosphere) as well as species to species interactions. Students will be able to trace the history of an interaction between man and the environment that demonstrates how human activities can deliberately or inadvertently alter the equilibrium in an ecosystem.

Sample Booktalk

Klass, David. California Blue. New York: Scholastic, 1994, IL YA, RL 6.3

John Rodgers is the star of his high school track team but is still unable to please his father. His father and brother are hometown football heroes who can't understand what John sees in track. John lives in lumber country where most of the town depends on the lumber industry for a livelihood. While John is in the woods, he comes upon a type of butterfly he's never seen. It turns out to be a new species of butterfly that needs to be protected. Now John faces a conflict between environmentalists and the townspeople who depend on the lumber industry. On top of all John's problems, he finds out his father has cancer. How will John handle all that is facing him? And what will the town decide about the butterflies? Will their livelihood take precedence over the environment?

Book List

Aronson, Billy. *Betting on Forever.* New York: Learning Triangle, 1997, IL 5-8, RL 4.8
  Strange-looking creatures from the past gather in their ghostly forms for an Extinct Animal Reunion where they discuss potential dangers to life on the planet.

George, Jean Craighead. *The Case of the Missing Cutthroats: An Eco Mystery.* New York: HarperTrophy, 1999, IL 5-8, RL 3.5
  After Spinner Shafter catches a cutthroat trout in the Snake River, she and her cousin Alligator search the nearby mountains to determine where the endangered fish came from and how it survived.

_____. *Frightful's Mountain*. New York: Dutton Children's Books, 1999, IL 5-8, RL 5.8
As she grows through the first years of her life in the Catskill Mountains of New York, a peregrine falcon called Frightful interacts with various humans, including the boy who raised her, a falconer who rescues her, and several unscrupulous poachers, as well as with many animals that are part of the area's ecological balance.

_____. *The Missing 'Gator of Gumbo Limbo: An Ecological Mystery*. New York: HarperTrophy, 1993, 1992, IL 5-8, RL 5.7
Sixth-grader Liza K., one of five homeless people living in an unspoiled forest in southern Florida, searches for a missing alligator destined for official extermination and studies the delicate ecological balance keeping her outdoor home beautiful.

_____. *The Talking Earth*. New York: Harper & Row, 1983, IL YA, RL 5.5
Billie Wind ventures out alone into the Florida Everglades to test the legends of her Indian ancestors and learns the importance of listening to the earth's vital messages.

Hobbs, Will. *Changes in Latitudes*. New York: Avon, 1993, 1988, IL YA, RL 7.5
A family trip to Mexico changes a cocky teenager's attitudes as he becomes exposed to his brother's consuming interest in saving endangered species, to his parents' problems, and to his own selfishness.

_____. *The Maze*. New York: Morrow Junior Books, 1998, IL 5-8, RL 4.2
Rick, a 14-year-old foster child, escapes from a juvenile detention facility near Las Vegas and travels to Canyonlands National Park in Utah where he meets a bird biologist working on a project to reintroduce condors to the wild.

Skurzynski, Gloria. *Wolf Stalker*. Washington, D.C.: National Geographic Society, 1997, IL 3-6, RL 5.5
Twelve-year-old Jack, his younger sister, and the family's teenage foster child, Troy, go to Yellowstone National Park. Here Jack's mother, a wildlife veterinarian, is investigating a report that wolves reintroduced to the park have killed a dog.

Sleator, William. *The Beasties*. New York: Dutton Children's Books, 1997, IL 5-8, RL 5.5
When 15-year-old Doug and his younger sister, Colette, move with their parents to a forested wilderness area, they encounter some weird creatures whose lives are endangered.

Taylor, Theodore. *The Weirdo*. San Diego: Harcourt Brace Jovanovich, 1991, IL YA
Seventeen-year-old Chip Clewt fights to save the black bears in the Powhaten National Wildlife Refuge.

Suggested Activities

Activity #6.1: It's Endangered

Have students research an endangered species such as the Karner Blue butterfly and write a one-page report outlining their findings.

Activity #6.2: Save the Earth

Have students create a poster reminding people of three simple things they can do every day to protect the environment. Hang the posters around the school.

Activity #6.3: Love Your Mother

Have students adopt the persona of Mother Earth to create a poem in three stanzas asking people to stop polluting her air, land, and water.

Activity #6.4: Animal Behavior

Have students make a two-column note-taker for animal behavior in the book and compare it to their knowledge of animal behavior from science studies (see Activity #6.4 Handout, page 36).

Activity #6.5: Needs of Endangered Animals

Have students create a graphic organizer depicting the needs of a particular endangered animal. What conditions of water, space, vegetation, food source, and safety from predators and pollution would the creature need to thrive? (see Activity #6.5 Handout, page 37).

Activity #6.6: The Right Stuff

Have students research what education and field experience it takes to become a wildlife veterinarian, wildlife biologist, or other wildlife professional.
Have them write their results in a resume.

Name _____ Date _____

Animal Behavior

In these two column notes, you will record scenes from the book that describe animal behavior and relate to your knowledge of animal behavior from your science studies.

Copy a quote from the book describing a particular behavior.	Write something you know from your science studies in relation to this behavior.
Copy a quote from the book describing a second example of animal behavior.	Write something you know from your science studies in relation to this behavior.
Copy a quote from the book describing a third example of animal behavior.	Write something you know from your science studies in relation to this behavior.

Name _____ Date _____

Endangered Species Needs

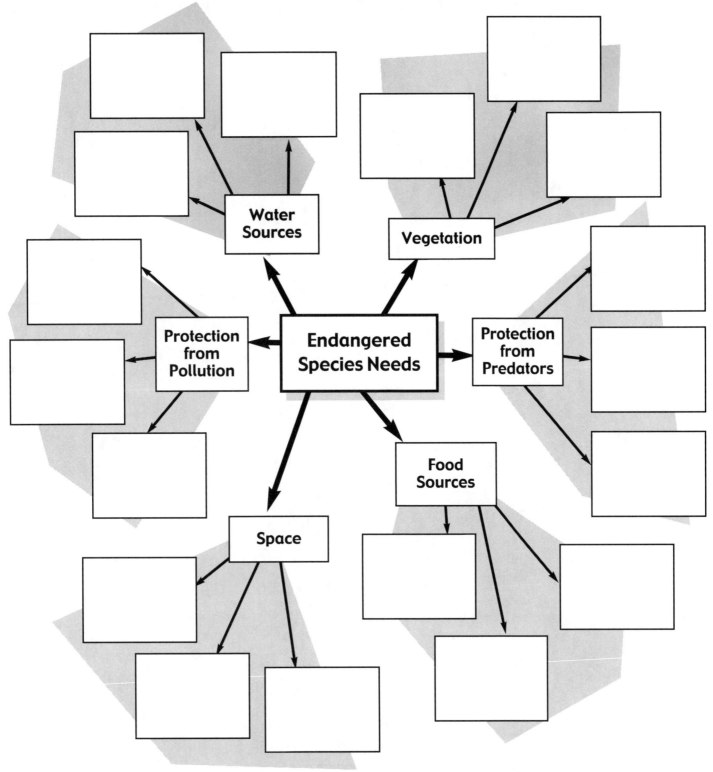

Chapter Seven

Oceanography

Introduction

The study of oceanography has long fascinated middle school students. They love to discover the exotic animals that live under the sea. There is a sense of mystery surrounding these creatures of the deep. But the study of oceans can extend beyond marine animals. The ocean is a vast, untapped resource scientists are now beginning to explore and utilize. In this chapter, we look at novels dealing with ocean creatures as well as the possibility of humans living under the oceans.

Standards Addressed

Students will identify and describe the basic requirements for sustaining life, e.g. plants and animals need food for energy and growth. They will describe how organisms can acquire energy directly or indirectly from the energy of the sun. They will understand the ocean environment and the animals and plants that depend on the ocean to sustain life.

Sample Booktalk

Bell, Hilari. *Songs of Power*. New York: Hyperion, New York: 2000, IL 5-8, RL 6.4

The underwater world is an incredible place to live. Imina doesn't quite share that opinion. She has come here reluctantly. She has been happy living with her grandmother while her parents were away doing their techie thing. They were important scientists who were trying to find an alternative way to feed the world's population since the traditional crops had failed. Grandmother, an Inuit shaman, was teaching Imina what she would need to know to become one also. Unfortunately, Grandmother died and now Imina finds herself living in a place with no magic—just science and technocrats. A terrible virus has destroyed most of the food supply around the world and now they must turn to the sea to feed billions of people worldwide. This station is just one of many that house scientists working on solving the problem of replenishing the oceans. Imina knows the work they do is important, but she just can't get too excited about it. When it becomes clear that someone is trying to sabotage the underwater habitat, Imina must call on her still undeveloped magic skills to try to save the colony.

Book List

Benchley, Peter. *Jaws*. New York: Fawcett Crest, 1992, 1974, IL YA
  This book recounts what happens when a great white shark terrorizes a small Long Island town.

Crichton, Michael. *Sphere: A Novel*. New York: Knopf, New York: 1987, IL YA
  A group of American scientists descend to the ocean floor to investigate a three-hundred-year-old spaceship of phenomenal dimensions, apparently undamaged by its fall from space. What will they find?

Hall, Elizabeth. *Venus Among the Fishes*. Boston: Houghton Mifflin, 1995, IL 5-8, RL 4.1
Coral and Snapper, two young dolphins, are sent to find help when their pod is attacked by orcas. Coral is captured by a group of humans doing marine research and spends several months with them. She then must decide whether to return to freedom or remain with her human trainer.

Heintze, Ty. *Valley of the Eels*. Austin, TX: Eakin Press, 1993, IL 5-8, RL 6.3
Young scuba divers Shawn and Billy follow a friendly dolphin to a domed installation in an ocean canyon where they meet a strange creature.

Hobbs, Valerie. *Tender*. New York: Frances Foster Books/Farrar, Straus and Giroux, 2001, IL YA
After her beloved Gran dies, 15-year-old Liv goes to California to live with the father she has never known and must adjust to his gruff ways and his life as an abalone diver, so different from her life in New York City.

Oceans of Magic. New York: DAW Books, 2001, IL YA
A collection of 13 stories by various authors about enchanted journeys on oceans and fantastical seas.

Powlik, James. *Sea Change*. New York: Island Books, 2000, 1999, IL YA
Renegade oceanographer Brock Garner teams up with Dr. Ellie Bridges in a race to discover a killer in the water after dead zones turn up in the Pacific Ocean and people begin to die.

Verne, Jules. *20,000 Leagues Under the Sea*. New York: Grosset & Dunlap, 1996, IL 5-8, RL 8.1
A 19th century science fiction tale in which a French professor and his companions, trapped aboard a fantastic submarine with a mad sea captain, come face to face with exotic ocean creatures and strange sights hidden from the world above.

Watts, Peter. *Starfish*. New York: Tor, 1999, IL YA
An international corporation develops a power facility at the bottom of the ocean and employs a bio-engineered crew to man it. Although the crew can withstand the underwater environment, it makes them so unstable that they are in danger of causing a deadly disaster.

Winton, Tim. *Blueback: A Contemporary Fable*. New York: Scribner, 1997, IL YA
Abel Jackson, a boy who lives with his mother in Longboat Bay, leaves home to become a scientist so he can learn the secrets of the sea. He discovers the ocean can take care of itself if man will simply leave it alone.

Suggested Activities

Activity #7.1: Help Wanted

Have students create a "Help Wanted" ad for a bio-engineered crew member for an underwater food generating plant. What abilities would the crew members need? Superhuman strength, the ability to go long periods without air, artificial limbs and lungs?

Activity #7.2: Dolphin Intelligence

Have students write and produce a skit in which a dolphin can talk to its trainer. What would the dolphin say? Would he choose to live in the safety of captivity or take his chances being free?

Activity #7.3: Life Under the Sea

What would it be like to live in an underwater civilization? Have students outline family life, education, jobs, recreation, and entertainment people would experience living under the sea (see Activity #7.3 Handout, page 42).

Activity #7.4: Shark Behavior

Have students research shark behavior, abilities, and temperament. Ask them to record their findings on a two-column note-taker to compare and contrast shark myth and reality (see Activity #7.4 Handout, page 43).

Activity #7.5: Whales and Dolphins

Have students research whales and dolphins. Have them learn about their capabilities and temperaments and create a chart that compares and contrasts the two animals (see Activity #7.5 Handout, page 44).

Activity #7.6: Listen to the Music

Have students listen to three recordings of whale sounds and imagine what the creatures are saying. Students can create lyric poems for each of three songs.

Activity #7.3 Handout: Life Under the Sea

Name _____ Date _____

Use this worksheet to organize your ideas of what life would be like living underwater.

Life Under the Sea

1. Family Life
- a
- b
- c

2. Education
- a
- b
- c

3. Jobs
- a
- b
- c

4. Recreation
- a
- b
- c

5. Entertainment
- a
- b
- c

Activity #7.4 Handout: Shark Behavior

Name _____ Date_____

Sharks

Research the abilities, temperament, and behavior of sharks. Record your findings on this two-column note-taker to compare and contrast shark myth and reality.

In this column, write statements that represent scientific facts about shark behavior. (e.g. a true statement about shark prey) 1. 2. 3.	In this column write statements of common beliefs about sharks. (e.g., sharks hunt people.) 1. 2. 3.

Activity #7.5 Handout: Whales and Dolphins

Name _____ Date _____

Whales and Dolphins

Whale Fact	Dolphin Fact	Similarities and Differences

Chapter Eight

Astronomy

Introduction

When we look into the night sky, we see possibilities. We see worlds we want to know about. Scientists have long been intrigued with the stars and planets around us. As new technologies are developed, we have the capability to learn more and more about space. The Hubble telescope has given us pictures of other worlds that have piqued our curiosity even more. The Mars Rover teased us into wanting more pictures of our neighbor. In this chapter, we read novels about the stars and other planets and our relationship with them.

Standards Addressed

Students will observe and describe the motion of the sun, moon, and stars from the perspective of the Earth. They will describe the characteristics of Earth and other planets in the solar system in terms of their ability to support life. They will identify the other planets in the solar system on a diagram or in the night sky, and describe their motions, as well as the motion of the planetary moons and comets. They will describe the interrelationships among the parts of an object or system.

Sample Booktalk

Latham, Jean Lee. *Carry On, Mr. Bowditch.* Boston: Houghton Mifflin, 1983, IL 5-8, RL 5.1

Have you ever wondered how sailors navigate by the stars? Is it some magic or secret only they know? How did sailors get where they were going before radar and radios? This is the story of Nat Bowditch. His father is a sea captain whose ship has gone down in a storm, leaving him penniless. The only way he can pay his bills is to have his son become an indentured servant. Young Nat is only 12; he must work as a servant until he is 21 in order to pay off his father's debts. Even this dire prospect doesn't deter Nat's natural curiosity. He works hard to educate himself. Fascinated with math and astronomy, he eventually becomes educated enough to become second mate in charge of his own duty. Nat goes on to study the stars and eventually becomes a famous astronomer and mathematician. This fictional biography shows us a man who realized his childhood desire to become a ship's captain and authored "The American Practical Navigator."

Book List

Barron, T. A. *Heartlight*. New York: Tor, 1994, IL 5-8, RL 6.2
  Kate and her grandfather use one of his inventions, which combines psychic power with quantum physics, to travel faster than the speed of light on a mission to save the sun from a premature death.

Crichton, Michael. *Sphere: A Novel*. New York: Ballantine, 1988, IL YA
  A group of American scientists descend to the ocean floor to investigate a three-hundred-year-old spaceship of phenomenal dimensions, apparently undamaged by its fall from space.

Flynn, Michael F. *Falling Stars*. New York: Tor, 2001, IL YA
When they learn that a series of asteroids are on a collision course with the planet, the members of the van Huyten family team up with the Pooles to try to save Earth from destruction.

Haldeman, Joe W. *The Coming*. New York: Ace Books, 2000, IL YA
Astronomy professor Aurora "Rory" Bell receives a message from outer space that leads her to believe extraterrestrial visitors are headed for Earth. By the time she decides the transmission may be a hoax, the media has taken over and will not let the story die.

Hickam, Homer H. *Back to the Moon*. New York: Delacorte, 1999, IL YA
Rocket engineer Jack Medaris has failed in his attempt to build a machine that would travel to the moon and collect an isotope desperately needed to produce energy on Earth. Hoping to redeem himself for what he sees as a personal failure, he highjacks the space shuttle Columbia and heads for the lunar surface.

Horton, Randy. *The Great UFO Frame-Up*. Buena Park, CA: Artesian, 2000, IL 5-8, RL 5.5
Jed hates his new astronomy class. He and his friend Pat come up with an idea to get out of class for the rest of the semester—a UFO abduction.

McDevitt, Jack. *Moonfall*. New York: HarperPrism, 1999, 1998, IL YA
In the year 2024 Vice President Charlie Haskell is at the new American Moonbase for its opening ceremonies when an amateur astronomer discovers a gigantic new comet headed straight towards the moon. With only five days until impact, it appears impossible to evacuate all personnel. Panic on Earth reaches epic proportions.

Rau, Dana Meachen. *One Giant Leap*. Norwalk, CT: Soundprints, 1996, IL 3-6, RL 4.8
While on a field trip to the National Air and Space Museum, Tommy imagines himself as Neil Armstrong, the mission commander aboard Apollo 11 and the first man to set foot on the moon.

Sturtevant, Katherine. *At the Sign of the Star*. New York: Farrar, Straus, and Giroux, 2000, IL 5-8, RL 6.3
In 17th century London, Meg, who has little interest in cooking, needlework, or other homemaking skills, dreams of becoming a bookseller and someday inheriting her widowed father's bookstore.

Warner, Gertrude Chandler. *The Outer Space Mystery*. Morton Grove, IL: Whitman, 1997, IL 3-6, RL 4.8
Henry, Jessie, Violet, and Benny, attending an astronomy conference with their grandfather at Mountvale College, become involved in a mystery when a student who is slated to make a presentation about an outer space discovery learns his research paper has been stolen.

Suggested Activities

Activity #8.1: Colony Design

Have students design a space colony. They will need to take into account where to put dining areas, sleeping quarters, workspaces, and recreation spaces.

Activity #8.2: Wanted: Professionals

What specific skills and occupations would be needed in a space colony? Have students choose six critically important professionals they would need in a space colony. Next, have them choose six classmates and list the skills they have that are needed by the particular profession for which they are chosen (see Activity #8.2 Handout, page 48).

Activity #8.3: Space Traveler Journal

Have students create a journal in which a space traveler on a long voyage writes to people she will never see again. What does she miss most? What are her hopes for lost love ones? What does she think she will find at her destination?

Activity #8.4: Future School

Have students create a floor plan for the school of the future. What will a typical classroom look like? What would the cafeteria, gym, and library look like?

Activity #8.5: This Is What I Need

Have students make a packing list of 10 items they would definitely take with them into space. Since space and weight limitations would be a reality, students will need to choose the lightest, smallest forms of the items, and justify each with a paragraph (see Activity #8.5 Handout, page 49).

Activity #8.6: Comic Book

Have students draw a comic book story of the first earth colony in a new galaxy (see Activity #8.6 Handout, page 50). As a follow-up activity, students could create a hypermedia presentation of the comic book story using a drawing program and a slide show program.

Name _____ Date _____

Wanted: Professionals

Profession	Candidate	Qualification

Activity #8.5 Handout: This Is What I Need

Name _____ Date _____

Packing List for Space Journey

Item	Size, Weight	Reason for Taking

Name _____ Date _____

Comic Book Storyboard

Use this sheet to create a draft of your storyboard. Plan what you will draw in each panel of your final copy, using stick figures and suggestions for dialogue.

Chapter Nine

Computers and Technology

Introduction

Just a few decades ago, no one could have imagined that the computer would be so much a part of our daily existence as it is in the 21st century. Computers are such an integral part of our daily lives that we may not even be aware of them. Computers run our microwave ovens as well as our heating and air conditioners. Computers even control the cars we drive and the public transportation we use. Technology now lets us purchase a personal transportation device called a Segway that will make walking obsolete! In this chapter, the novels deal with the pervasive nature of technology in our society.

Standards Addressed

Students will demonstrate an understanding of concepts underlying hardware, software, and connectivity, and of practical applications to learning and problem solving. They will apply strategies for identifying and solving routine hardware and software problems that occur during everyday use. They will understand how technology affects everyday life and be able to determine correct usage of computer technology.

Sample Booktalk

Westwood, Chris. *Virtual World*. New York: Viking, 1996, IL YA, RL 6.7

Kyle's dad wonders why kids don't go out and do stuff anymore. When he was a kid, they would play in the fields, go to the movies, or meet their friends on the street. What he doesn't seem to be able to understand is that there are no more fields nearby. You have to take a bus a long way to find some fields. And there are no movie theaters, either. They went out of business when movies went online. And forget about going out in the street. The streets are all run by gangs. Nope, what kids do nowadays is spend hours in front of the computer playing games. Really lucky ones get virtual reality equipment that lets them take it a step further.

Kyle and his friends are looking forward to the release of the latest game–Silicon Sphere. No one has seen it, but the hype is incredible. When his friend gets a pirated copy of the new game, Kyle and his friend Jack each take a copy of it to play. The first thing they notice is that it doesn't feel like an ordinary computer game. It seems as if it is part virtual reality because everything seems so real. Even after the game has exited, it's as if a piece of it is still with the boys. Jack even notices some sand in his room and remembers walking in sand in the game. But it's just a computer game. There is no way they can actually be entering the game, is there? Things like that just aren't possible. But still, when the game is on, it just seems so real…

Book List

Clarke, Arthur Charles. *2001: A Space Odyssey*. New York: New American Library, 1999, 1968 IL YA
  Accompanied by a navigator, three deep-freeze hibernauts, and the computer that guides him, David Bowman sets out in the spaceship Discovery to investigate a planet that may be inhabited by alien creatures.

Cray, Jordan. *Bad Intent*. New York: Aladdin Paperbacks, 1998, IL 5-8, RL 5.2
In order to increase his own status at Bloomfield High and win the affection of a pretty, popular cheerleader, Brian, the seemingly mild-mannered class president, allows his secret online identity to develop into something self-serving and dangerous.

Delaney, Mark. *The Vanishing Chip*. Atlanta: Peachtree, 1998, IL YA
When Mattie's grandfather becomes a suspect in the theft of a valuable computer chip, Peter, Byte, Jake, and Mattie, four high school students who consider themselves misfits, pool their talents to try to discover who really stole the chip and how.

Lorimer, Janet. *A Deadly Game*. Irvine, CA: Saddleback, 2001, IL YA
Jim Salvatori is hired to head up the newly created Computer Security Department at Mayfair College after the school's computer system is attacked by a virus. What people do not realize is that Jim is uniquely qualified to figure out whether Mayfair's computers fell victim to a joker or a criminal.

Manns, Nick. *Operating Code*. Boston: Little, Brown, 2001, IL 5-8, RL 5.8
Upon moving to Sentinel House, five-year-old Matty and 15-year-old Graham encounter ghosts from a nearby abandoned military compound. The real trouble begins when their father is arrested for posting information about a secret weapons system on the Internet.

Peck, Richard. *The Great Interactive Dream Machine: Another Adventure in Cyberspace*. New York: Dial Books for Young Readers, 1996, IL 5-8, RL 2.8
Josh Lewis is unwillingly drawn into the computer experiments of Aaron, his friend and fellow classmate, at an exclusive New York private school, and the two find themselves uncontrollably transported through space and time.

_____. *Lost In Cyberspace*. New York: Dial Books for Young Readers, 1995, IL 5-8, RL 5.4
While also dealing with changes at home, sixth-grader Josh and his friend Aaron use the computer at their New York prep school to travel through time, learning some secrets from the school's past and improving Josh's home situation.

Rendal, Justine. *A Very Personal Computer*. New York: HarperCollins, 1995, IL 5-8, RL 6.6
Twelve-year-old Pollard, an underachiever who is unhappy both at home and school, encounters a personal computer that addresses him by name and claims to be programmed to solve all his problems.

Scott, Melissa. *The Jazz*. New York: Tor, 2000, IL YA
Web site designer Tin Lizzy helps a teenage boy outrun the police and his parents after he steals a Hollywood studio's editing program to develop a sophisticated Web page.

Vande Velde, Vivian. *User Unfriendly*. San Diego: Magic Carpet Books, 2001, 1991, IL 5-8, RL 6.8
Fourteen-year-old Arvin and his friends risk using a computer-controlled role-playing game to simulate a magical world in which they actually become fantasy characters, even though the computer program is a pirated one containing unpredictable errors.

Suggested Activities

Activity #9.1: Safe Surfing

Have students create a set of guidelines for teen safety on the Internet. Have them suggest which places are "safe," what to do if you are frightened, and what information can safely be given out over the Net.

Activity #9.2: It's Your Turn

Have students create a plot outline for a role-playing game. They will need to include time, place, characters, a problem, and interesting details (see Activity #9.2 Handout, page 54).

Activity #9.3: Here's the Key

Computer keyboards are fairly standard. The letters of the alphabet are placed in the same positions as on typewriters of the past. Recently some keyboards have been ergonomically shaped. Many computers have instant Internet connection buttons. Ask students to design a keyboard that is more user-friendly. They could change the shape and position of the keys and add keys that would make keyboard use easier or more fun.

Activity #9.4: Web Page Design

Have students plan the design of a good, easy-to-navigate Web page for a sports team or favorite snack.

Activity #9.5: Cyber Society

Have students write a thought piece about the effect computers have on daily life. How have home life, work and school been affected by the presence and use of computers?

Activity #9.6: Then, Now, and Future

Students will research the capabilities and uses of computers both 50 years ago and today. Then they will brainstorm computers of the future and show their conclusions and ideas in a Venn diagram (see Activity #9.6 Handout, page 55).

Activity #9.2 Handout: It's Your Turn

Name _____ Date _____

Plot Outline

On the horizontal lines,
record events of the story

On the line at the top of the pyramid shape, write the
decision, discovery or event that determines the
resolution of the conflict.

Time:

Place:

Characters:

Problem:

Name _____ Date _____

Computers

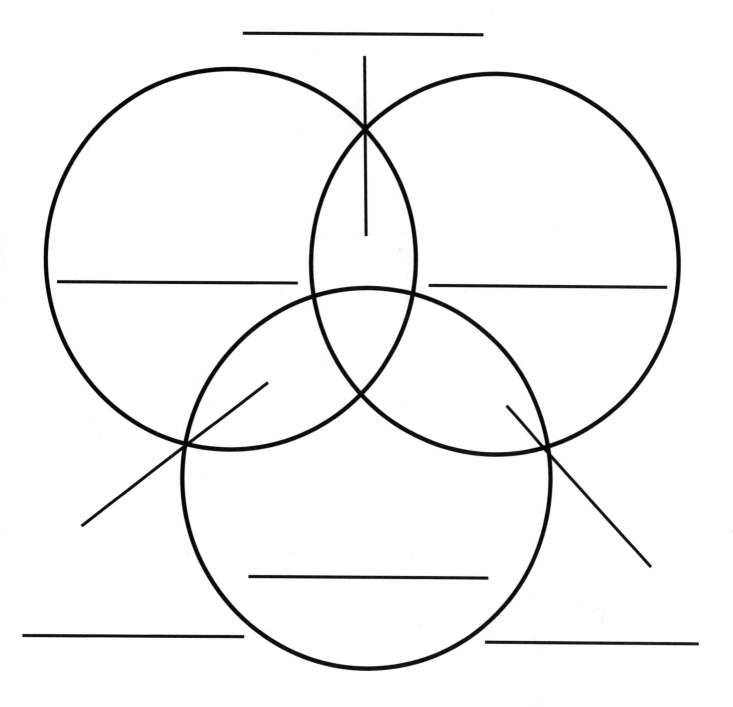

Chapter Ten
Medicine

Introduction

Mankind's search for cures from diseases goes further back than recorded history. Until relatively recent times, people used sometimes bizarre methods that today we know would never work. These days, we hear almost daily about a new cure or a promising treatment. But some "miracle" cures can do more harm than good. In this chapter, we examine novels that explore the ways in which people have dealt with diseases through the ages.

Standards Addressed

Students will demonstrate an increasing ability to understand fundamental structures, functions, and mechanisms of inheritance found in microorganisms, fungi, protists, plants, and animals. They will describe the major functions of the living cell and discuss how different groups of cells perform interrelated functions in any organism. They will describe the use of technology in the prevention, diagnosis, and treatment of disease, e.g. sanitation. medicines, organ transplants, adequate food and water supplies.

Sample Booktalk

Cushman, Karen. *Matilda Bone.* **New York: Clarion, 2000, IL 5-8, RL 6.1**

Deus misereatur. Matilda can't believe her eyes. This can't be the place that will be her new home. She has been raised in the Lord's manor and taught by Father Leufredus. She knows Latin, can read and write, and knows all the saints. Now, here she is at Blood and Bone Alley. This is a horrid place and Matilda is reluctant to find her new mistress. If she must assist a medical doctor, why can't it be someone like the famous Doctor Theobold? He is a real healer! But Matilda is left with Red Peg the Bonesetter, who specializes in broken bones, diseased limbs, sprains, and stiff joints. Matilda is appalled by all of it. She must deal with the horrid Doctor Margery, who is not really a doctor, Horanswith Leech, the bloodletter, and the kind Nathaniel Cross, the apothecary who is losing his eyesight. Can Matilda find her way in this new world? Will the saints she prays to help her? Or will she find that the trouble with saints is you never know what they'll say?

Book List:

Anderson, Laurie Halse. *Fever, 1793*. New York: Simon & Schuster Books for Young Readers, 2000, IL 5-8, RL 5.4
In 1793 Philadelphia, 16-year-old Matilda Cook, separated from her sick mother, learns about perseverance and self-reliance when she is forced to cope with the horrors of a yellow fever epidemic.

Avi. *Punch with Judy*. New York: Avon Books, 1997, 1993, IL 5-8, RL 5.6
An outcast eight-year-old boy, orphaned by the Civil War, is taken in by the owner of a traveling medicine show and, despite the doubts of others, years later he confirms the man's faith in him.

Cushman, Karen. *The Midwife's Apprentice*. New York: Clarion, 1995, IL YA
  In medieval England, a nameless, homeless girl is taken in by a sharp-tempered midwife. In spite of obstacles and hardship, she eventually gains the three things she most wants: a full belly, a contented heart, and a place in this world.

DeFelice, Cynthia C. *The Apprenticeship of Lucas Whitaker*. New York: Avon Books, 1998, 1996, IL 5-8, RL 5.5
  Twelve-year-old Lucas Whitaker, orphaned in 1849 when his entire family is claimed by consumption, takes a job as an apprentice with Doc Beecher and learns about the difference between superstition and science.

Dickinson, Peter. *Eva*. New York: Dell, 1990, IL YA, RL 7.0
  After a terrible accident, a young girl wakes up to discover she has been given the body of a chimpanzee.

Hesse, Karen. *A Time of Angels*. New York: Hyperion Books for Children, 2000, IL 5-8, RL 6.4
  Sick with influenza during the 1918 epidemic and separated from her two sisters, a young Jewish girl living in Boston relies on the help of an old German man, and her visions of angels, to get better and to reunite herself with her family.

Liles, Maurine Walpole. *Willer and the Piney Woods Doctor*. Austin, TX: Eakin Press, 1995, IL 5-8, RL 5.5
  To avoid being sent to an orphanage, 12-year-old Willer, who longs to know his parentage, agrees to work for a country doctor in Texas during the early 20th century.

Park, Barbara. *The Graduation of Jake Moon*. New York: Atheneum Books for Young Readers, 2000, IL 5-8, RL 6.3
  Fourteen-year-old Jake recalls how he has spent the last four years of his life watching his grandfather descend slowly but surely into the throes of Alzheimer's disease.

Rinaldi, Ann. *An Acquaintance with Darkness*. San Diego: Harcourt Brace, 1997, IL 5-8, RL 4.8
  When her mother dies and her best friend's family is implicated in the assassination of President Lincoln, 14-year-old Emily Pigbush must go live with an uncle she suspects of being involved in stealing bodies for medical research.

Thomas, Joyce Carol. *Marked by Fire*. New York: Avon Tempest, 1999, 1982, IL YA, RL 5.5
  Abby, born in an Oklahoma cotton field in the wake of a tornado, grows up learning the secrets of folk medicine from the healer Mother Barker.

Suggested Activities

Activity #10.1: Chicken Soup

Have students ask classmates and family members what is the best thing to do for a cold. They should then choose 10 of the answers and research their effectiveness. Have them report results on a graph created from a computer spreadsheet.

Activity #10.2: Alzheimer's

Recently, scientists have isolated the gene that causes early onset Alzheimer's disease. Have students research Alzheimer's disease and write about how it affects the daily life of its victims.

Activity #10.3: Perfect Baby

Genetic engineering is becoming a reality. Have students brainstorm the following: If you were about to become a parent and could ensure your child's genetic code, what would you choose for your child? Would you give the child strength, intelligence, and beauty or freedom from an illness or disability? Have students write a thoughtful piece defending their ideas.

Activity #10.4: Medical Miracles

Have students research the history of medical breakthroughs in the 20th century and present results in a detailed time line.

Activity #10.5: In Case of Accident

Have students research current first aid methods and create a picture book teaching simple first aid to younger children (see Activity #10.5 Handout, page 60).

Activity #10.6: Quilt

Have students create a Famous Scientists Quilt that incorporates original art depicting famous scientists like Lister, Pasteur, and Salk (see Activity #10.6 Handout, page 61).

Activity #10.5 Handout: In Case of Accident

Name _____ Date _____

In Case of Accident

Choose four accident scenarios such as a deep cut, choking, or broken bone, and sketch the first aid technique required.

1.

2.

3.

4.

Use the box below to sketch each of the scenes. (Reproduce the box as needed.)

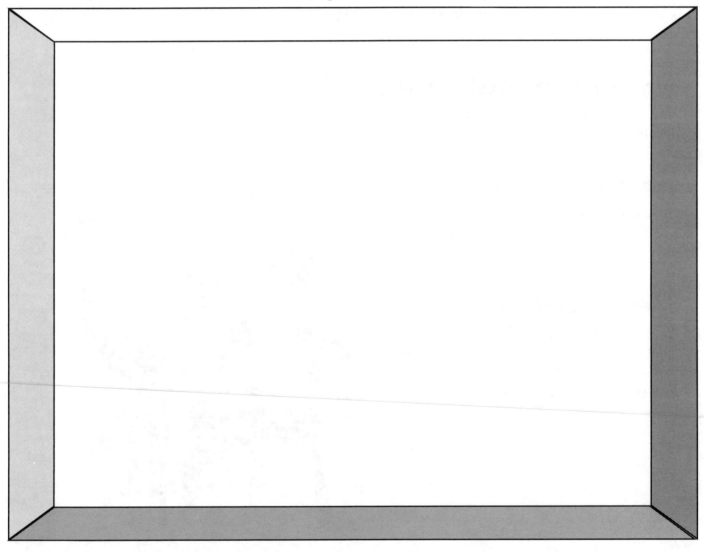

Now, color your pictures, cut them out, and arrange them in a booklet.

Activity #10.6 Handout: Quilt

Name _____ Date _____

Quilt Planner

When you're feeling ill, there's nothing like snuggling under a warm quilt. You will create a design for a quilt that will commemorate famous scientists whose discoveries have advanced the field of medicine. Your task is to choose six scientists like Joseph Lister and Marie Curie, write a paragraph on the discoveries of each, and create an original drawing of the scientist at work.

Scientist _____

Discovery _____

Description of the picture _____

_____

_____

_____

Scientist _____

Discovery _____

Description of the picture _____

_____

_____

_____

Scientist _____

Discovery _____

Description of the picture _____

_____

_____

_____

Scientist _____

Discovery _____

Description of the picture_____

_____

_____

_____

Scientist _____

Discovery _____

Description of the picture_____

_____

_____

_____

Scientist _____

Discovery _____

Description of the picture_____

_____

_____

_____

Index